CA Proficiency 2
Auditing and Assurance Toolkit

CA Proficiency 2
Auditing and Assurance Toolkit

Published in 2008 by
Institute of Chartered Accountants in Ireland
Burlington House, Burlington Road
Dublin 4

ISBN: 978-0-903854-52-8

Copyright of publication rests in entirety with the Institute of Chartered Accountants in Ireland (ICAI). All rights reserved. No part of this text may be reproduced or transmitted in any form or by any means, including photocopying, Internet or e-mail dissemination, without the written permission of the ICAI. Such written permission must also be obtained before any part of this document is stored in a retrieval system of any nature.

The opinions expressed in this publication are those of the author and do not necessarily represent the views of the ICAI. The text is designed to provide accurate and authoritative information in regard to the subject matter covered. It is sold on the understanding that the ICAI is not engaged in rendering professional services. If professional advice or other expert assistance is required, the services of a competent professional should be sought.

© *CA Proficiency 2 Auditing and Assurance Toolkit*, Institute of Chartered Accountants in Ireland, 2008

CONTENTS

	INTRODUCTION	1
SESSION 1	THE LEGAL AND BUSINESS ENVIRONMENT IN WHICH AUDIT AND ASSURANCE IS CONDUCTED	3
SESSION 2	THE PRINCIPLES OF AUDITING AND ASSURANCE IN SITUATIONS FREQUENTLY ENCOUNTERED IN PROFESSIONAL PRACTICE	7
SESSION 3	THE IMPACT OF THE AUDIT AND ASSURANCE ON THE CONTENT OF THE AUDIT REPORT ISSUED AT THE CONCLUSION OF THE AUDIT/ASSURANCE PROCESS	45
	SUGGESTED SOLUTIONS	49

PATHWAYS TO COMPETENCE IN AUDITING

BACKGROUND

You are James Crown and having completed your undergraduate degree you have been offered a training contract with Sonner & Saville, a Chartered Accountancy training firm. You have always wanted to be a CA and have always had your eye on getting a training contract with Sonner & Saville as it has the reputation of being a firm that will afford you a wide breadth of experience throughout the period of your training.

Jeanne Sonner is the managing partner, having taken over from her father who has now retired.

There are four other partners in the firm they are:

Kim Lu	Harry O'Neill	John Keane	Brenda Perry
Taxation	Corporate Finance	Audit	Financial Reporting
Partner	**Partner**	**Partner**	**Partner**

Your training will enable you to gain experience in all of these areas. When you arrived in Sonner & Saville you were pleased to see that Catherine Clarke, whom you knew vaguely from your student days, is also a trainee CA with the firm. As you both have completed relevant business degrees, the partners assume that you have a sound theoretical knowledge across the various disciplines.

In your first week in the office the partner's want you to just familiarise yourself with the Sonner & Saville way of doing business. They also take you, and because you already know her, Catherine to lunch. During lunch John Keane spoke on the merits on becoming a CA and emphasised at great length to you the relationship between your training and education. He knew that you would not be terribly busy this week and suggested that, you might, in the first instance read the Audit Competency statement published by the Institute and he reminded that you will need a strong theoretical understanding of the auditing theory to carry out your work during the period of your training contract. Have a read of the statement now – www.icai.ie

Welcome to the Pathways to Competence in Auditing Workbook. This Workbook consists of a number of tasks which will mirror the syllabus using a practical approach. At the end of the workbook, you will be part of an audit team who will have theoretically completed an audit, from the planning stage right through to the completion stage. You will be presented with a number of 'scenarios' during the audit which you will be required to resolve.

The workbook has been designed to imitate the real life experiences of a trainee chartered accountant in practice and also to help you to successfully pass the CAP 2 Auditing examination. Learning objectives and outcomes will be clearly stated for each task together with the expected 'competency level' (as per the Syllabus).

At the start of each session, the topic/subject will be clearly referenced to the relevant chapter in the course text book. Then at the end of the session, you will be directed to additional readings and questions. So now that you are all set, turn the page and commence the first session. Good Luck!

SESSION ONE
THE LEGAL AND BUSINESS ENVIRONMENT IN WHICH AUDIT AND ASSURANCE IS CONDUCTED

THE LEGAL AND BUSINESS ENVIRONMENT IN WHICH AUDIT AND ASSURANCE IS CONDUCTED

Learning Outcome:

At the end of this session you should be able to have an understanding and appreciation of the following:

- The respective responsibilities of directors and auditors in the context of corporate governance and statutory audit
- The related ethical and regulatory environment
- The auditing standard setting process
- The audit process

Competency Level Expected: U = Understanding

Competency at an understanding level is defined in the ICAI Competency Statement' as '*A comprehension of the fundamental concepts of the topic and an awareness of their impact in resolving problems*'. (See ICAI Competency, page 67)

Required Reading:

The following sections of the course text should be read prior to going further with this workbook:

CAP 2 (ICAI) Auditing – Chapter 1
Modern Auditing – Cosserat Chapters 1, 2, 3 and 4.

ES1: Integrity, Objectivity and Independence
ISA (UK and Ireland) 200: Objective and General Principles Governing an Audit of Financial Statements

Study the required reading to ensure you have an understanding of the above learning outcomes. Once you feel you understand the chapters, move on to Session 2.

SESSION TWO
THE PRINCIPLES OF AUDITING AND ASSURANCE IN SITUATIONS FREQUENTLY ENCOUNTERED IN PROFESSIONAL PRACTICE

THE PRINCIPLES OF AUDITING AND ASSURANCE IN SITUATIONS FREQUENTLY ENCOUNTERED IN PROFESSIONAL PRACTICE

Learning Outcome:

At the end of this session you should be able to have an understanding and appreciation of the following:

- The risk assessment process
- Assessment of specific systems of internal control with a view to identifying the critical risks and related controls
- Evidence gathering principles and procedures
- Selection and application of appropriate audit procedures to typical income statement and balance sheet account captions
- Selection and application of audit procedures to typical accounting estimates
- The framework for concluding on an area of audit work and the ability to draw appropriate conclusions based on a description of audit evidence available

Competency Level Expected: A = Application

Competency at an application level is defined in the ICAI Competency Statement' as *'A comprehension of the fundamental concepts*

of the topic and the ability to bring that comprehension to bear in resolving problems where data is provided in a structured form'.
(See ICAI Competency, page 67)

Required Reading:

The following sections of the course text should be read prior to going further with this workbook:

Cosserat Chapters 5,7,9,12,13,14,15,16

Relevant Chapters from ICAI Audit Manual

ISA (UK and Ireland) 230:	Documentation
ISA (UK and Ireland) 315:	Obtaining an Understanding of the Entity and its Environment and Assessing the Risks of material Misstatement
ISA (UK and Ireland) 320:	Audit Materiality
ISA (UK and Ireland) 330:	The Auditor's Procedures in Response to Assessed Risks
ISA (UK and Ireland) 500:	Audit Evidence
ISA (UK and Ireland) 501:	Audit Evidence – Additional Considerations for Specific Items
ISA (UK and Ireland) 505:	External Confirmations
ISA (UK and Ireland) 520:	Analytical Procedures
ISA (UK and Ireland) 540:	Audit of Accounting Estimates

Before you get started, answer the short-form questions overleaf. These will help you to familiarise yourself with the topic!

Short Form Questions

1. Suggest four instances where it is necessary for the auditor to exercise judgment during a statutory audit
2. State the alternative procedures available to an auditor where a debtor does not reply to a debtors confirmation letter
3. Detail four key procedures that an auditor should undertake during a stocktake
4. What four steps would you as an auditor take if, during the course of a statutory audit, you discovered that petty cash vouchers were being approved in advance by the financial controller

5. Give four examples of tests of control procedures that an auditor may adopt in obtaining evidence about the effective operation of internal controls over fixed assets
6. Identify four factors which influence the reliability of audit evidence
7. In the audit of accounting estimates, state four steps in the review and testing of the process used by the management or the directors of the company
8. State four quality control procedures that an auditor may adopt
9. State four procedures that an auditor should carry out as part of his review of the accounting policies adopted by a client company
10. State two steps you would carry out to satisfy yourself as to the existence of stocks held by third parties. State two steps you would carry out in respect of the valuation of stocks held by third parties
11. Set out four procedures you would undertake to ensure that a company maintains proper books and records
12. Outline four procedures which an auditor should adopt in respect of a detailed profit and loss account for inclusion as the final pages of a set of financial statements
13. Set out four audit considerations in respect of the audit of the VAT balances in the accounts of a client organisation
14. State two factors that must be considered in determining sample size. State two benefits to an auditor of using statistical sampling
15. State four audit procedures you would undertake to ensure completeness of sales and debtors

Section 2.1

You are now in your second year in Sonner & Saville. You note from the planning board that you are commencing an audit next Monday of Steelx Limited. On the team are the following:

Louise Clark – senior
James Crown – semi-senior
Mathew Murphy – junior

Since you are not booked on anything this week, you approach Louise and ask her is there is anything you can do. Louise is delighted you are free since she is extremely busy finishing another assignment. She asks you to prepare a memorandum for inclusion in the planning section noting the following:

- Set materiality and its basis
- Carry out preliminary analytical review of the trial balance
- Identify the critical areas for our audit
- Determine if we should use a systems based or risk based audit approach

In order to help you with the planning, she hands you the minutes of the planning meeting which took place between partner, manager, senior and client.

Steelx Limited
Planning Meeting
23rd February 2008

In Attendance: John Keane   -   Partner
                 Louise Clark -   Senior
                 Ed Burke   -   MD
                 Mark Power   -   FD

- The company was formed on 11th March 1994 by Ed and Carmel Burke. The company has grown from strength to strength in the last 13 years.
- The principal activity is the sale of steel. The year end is 31 December 2007. You were appointed auditors on 16th December 2007.
- The company is now too large for their existing auditors and they have decided on Saville & Sonner as they promised to undertake a very efficient audit with an experienced team.
- Ed is the MD and Carmel is a director but not involved in the running of the business
- The company employs 23 people split as follows:
    - Management   3
    - Finance   3
    - IT   1
    - Sales   6
    - Warehouse   10

- The stock count was attended by Saville and Sonner. 20 items from the floor to the sheet and 20 items from the sheet to the floor were counted. No material errors were noted
- The finance team is headed by Mark Power, the Finance Director. He has a financial controller Paula Flynn reporting to him who in turn has a team of 2 part qualified accountants working in the finance department.
- Mark was appointed as Finance Director in the company 4 months ago – the company was growing and Ed knew that there was a need for a director in the finance department who would assist him in growing the company. Paula never finished her ACA qualifications and is not fully qualified, however she is good at managing the day to day administration of the accounting department. Ed really never knew what the financial state of the company was until the audited accounts were finalised and now wanted better information from the finance department.
- Mark has been trying to implement a monthly reporting systems since he started. This however has proven difficult since due to the volume of transactions, and Paula's workload, balances were only reconciled at year end for the auditors. He was shocked when he saw the number of audit adjustments that were posted in the previous year. He has worked very closely with Paula over the last 4 months in order to get the trial balance accurate at the year end and to have minimal audit adjustments.
- After the audit, Paula is going to prepare monthly management accounts for Mark who will then present them to the board
- The company uses Accounting I an Accounting Software Package, and Mark has noted that if the company continues to grow, he will have to consider installing a more advanced system.
- Mark presented the trial balance for the year end
- He is confident that the trial balance is fairly accurate and does not expect many audit adjustments. During the discussions, the following was noted:
  - Fixed asset additions are quite high due to the purchase of new motor vehicles and forklifts during the year. Additions are depreciated from the date of acquisition
  - There is no fixed asset capitalization policy – all invoices are approved by Ed and he decides whether to capitalize or not.

- The client maintains a fixed asset register on excel.
- Two cars were disposed of during the year – these were sold to the employees for €3k each. This money has been received into the bank.
- An adjustment had to be made to the stock value in the system of €100k compared with physical stock. This has concerned Mark and he intends to monitor the monthly system vs actual stock figures very closely in the coming months.
- There are two large accruals:
  - €150k for rebates payable to customers – the company has agreements with certain customers once they achieve a particular level of sales
  - Bonus accrual which is based on the profit for the year – this will not be paid until after the issue of final financial statements
- Two employees injured on site during the year – the payment of their claims have still to be resolved. Currently no accrual has been posted since they presume it will be covered by their insurance
- Mark has hired a credit controller in the last month to concentrate on getting cash from debtors. Though the level of cash received is good, Mark noted a lot of old balances sitting on the ledger – Ed thinks that these should be recoverable. Mark states that at the time of fieldwork, the credit controller will have a good handle on the listing and will be able to indicate whether the balances need to be provided
- Mark admitted that wages are in a bit of a mess – they had not been reconciled since the last audit and time constraints has not allowed him to look at these in detail. He hopes to have them fully reconciled by the audit.
- Mark said the outlook of the company is good. 2008 was a good year, however, in the midst of an economic slowdown, the current growth rate is not expected to continue.

There being no other business, the meeting ended

Louise Clark
24/02/08

Steelx Limited

TRIAL BALANCE for the year 1/1/07 to 12/31/07

	Debit €/£	Credit €/£	Comparative €/£
Sales		15,425,063.00	−14,132,302.50
Opening stock - finished goods	1,095,578.00		754,735.50
Cost of sales	14,214,284.00		11,687,415.00
Closing stock - finished goods		1,210,734.00	−1,095,578.00
Rent	183,780.00		221,661.00
Rates, light and heat	57,792.50		43,855.50
Insurance	24,987.00		12,487.00
Repairs and maintenance	78,654.00		24,687.00
Wages and salaries	952,304.00		805,356.00
Staff PRSI	46,257.00		40,987.00
Staff pension contributions	44,181.00		131,013.00
Motor expenses	44,854.00		40,025.00
Travel and subsistence	17,799.00		20,653.00
Telephone	35,915.00		35,659.00
Distribution costs	245,781.00		124,687.00
Sundry warehouse expenses	16,915.50		12,843.50
Printing, stationery and postage	19,528.00		17,414.00
Staff training	3,556.50		2,432.00
Computer costs	14,567.00		12,457.00
Subscriptions and donations	10,310.00		3,542.00
Canteen	7,886.00		8,242.00

Steelx Limited

TRIAL BALANCE for the year 1/1/07 to 12/31/07 (Continued)

	Debit €/£	Credit €/£	Comparative €/£
Provision for doubtful debts	20,000.00		0.00
Bank charges	12,726.50		11,639.00
Legal and professional fees	33,372.50		40,327.00
Auditors remuneration	21,487.00		14,578.00
Depreciation of plant and machinery	35,771.00		50,057.00
Depreciation of motor vehicles	52,393.00		44,805.00
Depreciation of computer equipment	1850		251
Bank interest payable	21,408.50		101,104.00
Corporation tax charge	0.00		80,163.00
Plant and machinery	312,604.00		447,199.00
P & M - Additions @ cost	131,809.00		18,793.00
P & M - Disposals @ cost		0	−39,915.00
P & M - Accumulated depn		174,776.00	−246,309.00
P & M - Depn on disposals		0	39,915.00
P & M - Depn charge		35,771.00	−50,057.00

Motor Vehicles	127,353.00		64,703.00
Mtr Veh - Additions @ cost	85,483.00		62,650.00
Mtr Veh - Disposals @ cost		23,787.00	0
Mtr Veh - Accumulated depn		55,086.00	−2,696.00
Mtr Veh - Depn on disposals	21,805.00		0
Mtr Veh - Depn charge		52,393.00	−44,805.00
Computer equipment	20,743.00		52,695.00
Equip - Additions @ cost	3,484.00		0
Equip - Disposals @ cost		0	−23,216.00
Equip - Accumulated depn		20,445.00	−52,444.00
Equip - Depn on disposals	0		23,216.00
Equip - Depn charge		1850	−251
Finished goods	1,210,734.00		2,191,156.00
Trade debtors	930,123.00		1,032,982.00
Provision for doubtful debts		20,000.00	0.00
Prepayments and accrued income	127,344.00		57,628.00
Cash at bank	1,019,369.00		692,863.00
Trade creditors		1,290,391.00	−1,384,832.83
Corporation tax	142,541		−71,759.00
PAYE and PRSI		6,176.00	5,612.00
VAT liability		233,326.00	−315,316.00

Steelx Limited

TRIAL BALANCE for the year 1/1/07 to 12/31/07 (Continued)

	Debit €/£	Credit €/£	Comparative €/£
Accruals and deferred income		259,049.00	180,672.00
Ordinary share capital brought forward		15,000.00	−15,000.00
Profit and loss account brought forward		2,623,483.00	−1,738,678.00
	21,447,330	21,447,330	590,522

Section 2.2   Fixed Assets

The audit of Steelx Limited has now commenced and you, with your other two team members, are now on site.

Louise has asked you to complete the fixed asset section of the audit file and hands you the following:

- Client fixed asset register
- Invoices relating to additions
- Summary of repairs and maintenance nominal as prepared by client. You had asked in your planning letter than the client extracts invoices over the value of €10k
- Fixed asset audit programme which she has used on previous audits – she feels it is appropriately tailored for use on the audit of Steelx Limited

Steelx Ltd.
Kylemore Industrial Estate
Dublin

Mayday Motors
1 Main Street
Athlone
Co. Westmeath

Date: 01/08/2007

Invoice Number: 17983

Description	Quantity	Price
Combilift Forklift S/N 8483	1	£/€41,100.00
VAT at 21%		8,631
Total		£/€49,731

VAT registration number: 425656

Steelx Ltd.
Kylemore Industrial Estate
Dublin

Mayday Motors
1 Main Street
Athlone
Co. Westmeath

Date: 01/02/2007

Invoice Number: 17883

Description	Quantity	Price
Combilift Forklift S/N 8483	1	£/€71,500.00
VAT at 21%		15,015
	Total	£/€86,515.00

VAT registration number: 425656

Steelx Ltd.
Kylemore Industrial Estate
Dublin

Mayday Motors
1 Main Street
Athlone
Co. Westmeath

Date: 01/10/2007

Invoice Number: 19873

Description	Quantity	Price
Ford Focus Van	1	£/€11,983
VAT at 21%		2,517
	Total	£/€14,500

VAT registration number: 425656

Steelx Ltd.
Kylemore Industrial Estate
Dublin

Mayday Motors
1 Main Street
Athlone
Co. Westmeath

Date: 01/09/2007

Invoice Number: 19872

Description	Quantity	Price
Toyota Avensis	2	£/€49,000
VAT at 21%		10,290
	Total	£/€59,290

VAT registration number: 425656

Steelx Ltd.
Kylemore Industrial Estate
Dublin

Mayday Motors
1 Main Street
Athlone
Co. Westmeath

Date: 10/01/2008

Invoice Number: 12356

Description	Quantity	Price
Mazda	1	£/€24,500.00
Vat at 21%		5,145
	Total	£/€29,645.00

VAT registration number: 425656

FIXED ASSET WORK PROGRAMME

Client: Prepared By:

Year Ended: Reviewed By:

                             Date:

Procedure	Reference
1. Cast the fixed asset subsidiary ledgers and agree the total with the general ledger accounts. Prepared a fixed asset lead schedule	
2. Scan the repairs and maintenance account items for reasonableness, noting any large or unusual items.	
3. Obtain, prepare or update a permanent file schedule summarising the fixed asset capitalisation policies and review for appropriateness and consistency of accounting method with the prior year.	

4. Identify significant fixed assets additions:
  a) Examine appropriate supporting documents.
  b) Ensure that VAT has been properly accounted for
  c) Ensure additions have been recorded correctly	

5. Review all material disposals of assets and examine appropriate supporting documents. Ensure that the profit/loss on disposal are calculated correctly and disposal is recorded correctly.	
6. Determine whether depreciation or amortisation charged to profit and loss account is calculated on a consistent and reasonable basis.	

Fixed Asset Register (£/€)

Asset Code	Description	Date of addition/ disposal	Life	Opening cost	Additions/ (Disposals)	Closing Cost	Opening Dep	YTD Depn	Disposal	Closing Depn	Closing NBV
COMPUTER EQUIPMENT											
821	Server			19,876		19,876	19,876			19,876	–
859	SCANNER/ SOFTWARE	01/06/2007	2		3,484	3,484		1,742		1,742	1,742
778	/KEYBOARD/ MONITOR		8	867		867	569	108		677	190
Total				20,743	3,484	24,227	20,445	1,850		22,295	1,932
MOTOR VEHICLES											
834	HYUNDAI SONATA		2	17,089		17,089	8,545	8,545		17,089	–
920	FORD FOCUS VAN	01/10/2007	4		11,983	11,983	0	749		749	11,234
832	BMW 528i		2	21,775		21,775	10,888	10,887		21,775	–
833	VOLVO	01/11/2007	2	13,473	(13,473)	0	6,736	5,614	(12,350)	0	–
835	VOLVO	01/11/2007	2	10,314	(10,314)	0	5,157	4,298	(9,455)	0	–
836	BMW 325i		4	64,703	0	64,703	23,761	16,176		39,937	24,766
888	TOYOTA AVENSIS	01/09/2007	4		24,500	24,500		2,042		2,042	22,458
889	TOYOTA AVENSIS	01/09/2007	4		24,500	24,500		2,042		2,042	22,458
890	MAZDA	10/01/2008	4		24,500	24,500		2,042		2,042	22,458
Total				127,354	61,696	189,050	55,087	52,395	(21,805)	85,676	103,374

Fixed Asset Register (£/€) (Continued)

Asset Code	Description	Date of addition/ disposal	Life	Opening cost	Additions/ (Disposals)	Closing Cost	Opening Dep	YTD Depn	Disposal	Closing Depn	NBV
PLANT & MACHINERY											
858	WAREHOUSE RACKING	02/02/2007	8.000000		9,659	9,659	–	1,207		1,207	8,452
860	COMBILIFT FORKLIFT S/N 8483	01/08/2007	5.000000		47,100	47,100	–	9,420		9,420	37,680
740	SHELVING		8.000000	6,819		6,819	2,879	492		3,371	3,447
757	OFFICE FURNITURE		8.000000	28,502		28,502	17,873	1,329		19,202	9,300
758	PHONE SYSTEM		8.000000	4,190		4,190	1,287	363		1,650	2,540
768	CHANNELS FOR MATERIAL STORAGE		8.000000	6,399		6,399	4,276	265		4,541	1,857
770	CONF. ROOM FURNITURE		8.000000	2,506		2,506	1,200	163		1,363	1,143
775	FORK LIFT RAMP		8.000000	6,031		6,031	2,761	409		3,170	2,861
783	PAINTING OF RACKING		8.000000	18,720		18,720	14,233	561		14,794	3,926
790	BEAM SAW AP		5.000000	41,062		41,062	5,128	7,187		12,315	28,747
810	CANON IR2010F FAX MACHINE		5.000000	3,000		3,000	1,654	269		1,923	1,077
746	CARPETS NEW BUILDING		8.000000	14,360		14,360	8,374	748		9,122	5,238
747	ELECTRICAL FITTINGS		8.000000	25,490		25,490	19,082	801		19,883	5,607
750	LEASEHOLD IMPROVEMENTS		12.000000	82,578		82,578	64,234	1,529		65,763	16,816
752	LEGAL FEES ASSET 5750		8.000000	3,054		3,054	1,267	223		1,490	1,563
756	WIRING/ DATA POINTS		8.000000	11,428		11,428	5,679	719		6,398	5,030

PRINCIPLES OF AUDITING AND PROFESSIONAL PRACTICE 27

ID	Description	Date	Rate	Cost Opening	Additions	Cost Closing	Acc Dep Opening	Charge	Disposals	Acc Dep Closing	NBV
759	BLINDS (ALL OFFICES)		8.000000	1,016			543	59		602	414
763	ALARM SYSTEM		8.000000	8,215			4,212	500		4,712	3,503
794	ELECTRICAL WORK		8.000000	6,392			2,091	538		2,629	3,763
795	ELECTRICAL WORK		8.000000	1,181			789	49		838	343
799	ADD CABLING & DATA POINTS		8.000000	2,502			1,298	150		1,448	1,053
801	STAIRS TO ROOF AREA		8.000000	3,275			1,290	248		1,538	1,737
802	LIFTING TABLE FOR ROOF AREA		8.000000	1,250			374	110		484	767
806	ELECTRICAL WORK (WAREHOUSE)		8.000000	1,210			289	115		404	806
807	ELECTRICAL WORK (WAREHOUSE)		8.000000	1,414			309	138		447	967
782	MATERIALS & MOVEMENT FLT BATT		8.000000	4,000			1,709	286		1,995	2,005
784	FORKLIFT PARTS		8.000000	5,700			2,767	367		3,134	2,567
789	FORKLIFT TRUCK AP		3.000000	6,266			2,398	1,289		3,687	2,579
812	JUNGHEINRICH FLT OVERHAUL		5.000000	7,543			4,390	631		5,021	2,523
813	80V BATTERIES CESAB SDTRACKER		5.000000	8,500			2,390	1,222		3,612	4,888
861	COMBILIFT FORKLIFT	01/02/2007	5.000000		71,500	71,500		14,300		14,300	57,200
919	FORK LIFT 48V BATTERY	01/01/2007	5.000000		3,550	3,550		710		710	2,840
	Total			312,604	131,809	444,413	174,776	46,398	—	221,174	
	Grand Total			460,699	136,746	597,446	195,221	90,014	—	232,842	

Repairs and Maintenance Summary	€/£	
Homebase - Batteries	65	
JK Office fitters	13,768	*invoice attached*
Homebase - Lamp	24	
Kleenze - Cleaning of warehouse	675	
Power hose	197	
Furniture for you	17,980	*invoice attached*
Stones & All - Gravel for site	1,947	
PMAC Motor repairs - Forklift repairs	9,978	
PMAC Motor repairs - Fleet repairs	9,347	
Warehouse general	9,673	
Accrual for factory repairs	15,000	
	78,654	

Steelx Ltd.
Kylemore Industrial Estate
Dublin

JK Office Fitters
1 Donegall Place
Belfast

Date: 23/02/2007

Invoice Number: 13768

Description	Quantity	Price €/£
Labour on fit-out of new reception		13,768
VAT at 21%		2,891
	Total	16,659

VAT registration number: 123456

Steelx Ltd.
Kylemore Industrial Estate
Dublin

Furniture For You
11-13 O'Connell Street
Limerick
Co. Limerick

Date: 03/03/2007

Invoice Number: 17980

Description	Quantity	Price
Reception fit-out	1	€/£17,980
VAT at 21%		3,776
	Total	€/£21,756

VAT registration number: 187314

Task 2.2.1

Complete the audit programme for fixed assets. Conclude with a file note to Louise detailing any points for discussion and potential audit adjustments.

Task 2.2.2

Using your experience, note any additional tests you feel should be included in the audit work programme. For each test, briefly note the audit work you would carry out on each test

Section 2.3   Stock

The stock count was attended by a semi-senior Sophie Donovan, who is now on study leave. You have given Matthew the stock attendance results and asked him to compare to the final stock sheets. While doing this work, he indicates that there are numerous differences between count sheets and final sheets. You have asked him to get a comment from the stock manager as to the reason for the differences. Mathew has now done as much as he can and has handed you his workpaper below:

Client name: Steelx Limited
PERIOD END: 31-Dec-2007
PERFORMED BY: Matthew Murphy

Item number	Ticket No.	Location	Quantity per Stock Count	Size	Quantity per final stock sheets	Difference	Note
14608	1363	SA1	1298	3000mm	1408	−110	1
22177	1506	RB1	1920	832.2mm	1920	0	
22177	1507	RB1	1970	832.2mm	1970	0	
11062	1395	TB1	2106	3000mm	2106	0	
15581	3538	KJ2	1140	777mm	1140	0	
22653	3222	T/RACK/E	1038	3000mm	1038	0	
14608	1329	VB1	378	3000mm	1070	−692	2
14608	1331	VB1	1678	3000mm	1058	620	3
5603	1004	LJ3	1310	1000mm	1310	0	
17083	3205	UA1	964	706.8mm*875.2mm	964	0	
12275	3560	CD5	694	42mm*12mm	694	0	

17083	3211	UA1	425	706.8mm*875.2mm	873	−448	4
18886	1899	MH1	660	2000mm	660	0	
22826	3252	TA8	549	3000mm	962	−413	5
18886	3901	MH1	512	2000mm × 1000mm × 1.2mm	512	0	
			18728			**−1043**	

Note 1 110 sheets of this steel had been despatched to a customer the day before the stock count. However, these were the incorrect width and were returned before the year end. The new steel was not despatched until after the year end

Note 2 The warehouse is pushed for space, and as a result, some stock items are held at third party stock-holding location - the remainder of this steel is located there

Note 3 Part of this steel was custom made for a particular customer, however, the customer did not require the full quantity - the related stock is therefore considered obsolete and has not been included in the final stock

Note 4 These items were ready to be despatched to a customer in the first week of the new year, and therefore had been set aside during the stock count - they were therefore not included in the count. The order was received on 02/01/08 before the ledgers were closed off.

Note 5 The stock manager cannot explain this difference - he assumes it was error on the part of the firm representative that they did not count all areas which included this steel.

Task 2.3.1

Create a workpaper identifying actions you would take, and audit work you would carry out, for each of the identified discrepancies. Give it to Louise for approval before you proceed.

Task 2.3.2

Matthew is very keen to learn and is continually asking you questions. He has yet to carry out a stock take and on completing the workpaper for you above, is curious as to why the counts are done both from the sheet to the floor and from the floor to the sheet. He is glad he is looking at a stock section before he ever has to do a stock count because his peers are saying that they are being sent out on stock counts and do not have a clue what to do. Write a short memo for Matthew detailing why two-way counts are carried out on a stock count.

Task 2.3.3

Over lunch you mention to Louise that the juniors have very little knowledge of the stock count procedure. Having done a lot of stock counts as a junior, you ask Louise why staff are never given a work programme. Louise replies that there used to be one years ago but it has just been ignored in recent years. Seniors simply instruct staff to count a particular amount of items, collate on an excel spreadsheet and write a brief report on the stock count procedures.

You are back in the office that evening picking up files and you see that John Keane is still in his office. You pop in to voice your concerns over the stock count procedures and suggest that you create a stock count audit procedure worksheet. John is delighted and notes that as a firm they need to tighten up on procedures surrounding the stock counts carried out by the firm. You tell John you will send him a draft work programme for review by the end of the week.

Prepare a stocktake attendance programme.

Task 2.3.4

You ask Matthew to carry out the price testing of the stock. Since he has never done this before, he looks at you blankly and admits that he doesn't understand what exactly he is supposed to be doing. Set out, in bullet point format, for Matthew how he should carry out the pricing tests, indicating the reasoning behind them.

Section 2.4 Creditors and Accruals

Louise has handed you the accruals listing and back-up received from Paula – the accountant. She states that though you probably have not done an accruals section before, it will be good experience. Also, since you did the planning, you know the company well.

Steelx Limited

Accruals

	€/£	
Audit fees	12,000	as agreed
Employers liability insurance	15,000	invoice attached
Rebates	150,000	as per MD
Bonus accrual	35,000	as per MD
Goods received not invoiced	32,049	
Factory repairs	15,000	repairs to commence April 08
	259,049	

Steelx Ltd. P Shay Insurers
Kylemore Industrial Estate Safe Street
Dublin Dublin

Date: 01/01/2008

Invoice Number: 19872

Description	Quantity	Price
Annual insurance renewal for period 01/01/07 to 31/12/07. Employers liability insurance with customer excess of €50,000 **Invoice over-due. Please pay on receipt**		£/€15,000
	Total	£/€15,000

Task 2.4.1

You go straight to Mark to discuss the largest accrual – the rebate accrual. He states that Ed, the MD calculates the rebate accrual himself based on agreed rates with customers. Customers get a rebate once they reach certain sales value. However, these rebates are historical and Mark cannot find any agreements. Ed does not want the customers to be contacted in case they demand an increase in the rebate %. Mark also notes that this accrual has been building up for a number of years – Ed does not pay the rebates until the customers looks for it.

Outline the audit work you would carry out on the accruals schedule.

With regard to the rebate and bonus accrual outline what further information/audit evidence you would require from the management of Steelx Limited. Bring any potential audit adjustments to the audit and adjustment schedule.

Task 2.4.2

You ask Matthew to audit the creditors' reconciliations. He tells you that he has not audited creditors' reconciliations before and is unsure how to do it, and why we do it. As usual, Matthew's inquisitive mind needs to understand why he is doing something. You are under pressure, and start to quickly explain to him, however, as you are talking you see the look of confusion on his face. You agree to write a file note at home tonight explaining the following:

- The purpose of creditors' reconciliations
- Why they are required
- How to audit them.

And you tell him that he can do them tomorrow.

Write a file note explaining creditors reconciliations identifying all three points above.

Task 2.4.3

Matthew comes to you with a supplier reconciliation that he is having difficulty with. He says the majority of the reconciliations simply agreed statement to listing, however this particular one is confusing him:

Fabri Steel Limited

Balance per accounts payable listing				64,875
Balance per supplier statement				101,582
Difference				36,707
Reconciled by:				
December payment run not on statement			– 7,800	
Invoices on statement not on ledger:				
29/12/2007	inv 14255	7,001		
30/12/2007	inv 15487	18,123		
30/12/2007	inv 15488	6,925		
30/12/2007	inv 15489	12,458		
			44,507	
				36,707
				—

Outline for Matthew the audit work he should carry out on the above reconciliation.

Task 2.4.4

Matthew has come across some supplier balances which do not have any statements. Indicate to Matthew the alternative audit work he should carry out.

Section 2.5 Debtors and Prepayments

Task 2.5.1

You get a phone call from John commending your efforts on the stock attendance audit programme that you completed. He is very happy with it and the audit technical partner is just making a few changes before it is issued to the audit department for use. Louise also hears from John how well you have done. She tells you that on her last job, John had a lot of review points on the debtors section since she did not have enough tests in her audit programme. She asks you to prepare a draft of the audit programme for the debtors and prepayments section of Steelx Limited

Task 2.5.2

You ask Matthew to do a workpaper on the prepayments. Once completed, he gives it to you for your review:

Steelx Limited	**Prepared by**	MM
Prepayments	**Reviewed by**	
	Date	
	£/€	
Rates	34,568	prepayment recalculated
Insurance	26,700	discussed with client - appears reasonable
Systems maintenance	11,200	contract was due for renewal in November 2007 - the company has entered discussions to renew the contract - prepayment appears reasonable
Miscellaneous	54,876	all prepayments below €10k - no further work required
	127,344	

Prepare a review comment schedule for Matthew to complete the audit of prepayments following your review of the workpaper.

Task 2.5.3

Louise asks you to audit the ageing of debtors and potential bad debt provision. You ask the credit controller for an ageing of debtors and an analysis of all debtors greater than 90 days. You get the following workpaper:

	€/£'000
Current	200
30 days	154
60 days	90
90 days	350
120 days	200
Unallocated cash	– 64
	930
bad debt provision	20,000

Debtors greater than 90 days:

Customer No	Balance	Comment
1264	15,487	received post year end
1654	65,487	taking legal action to pursue payment
1687	164,587	company in liquidation
1876	45,187	received post year end
1248	49,876	incorrect pricing - credit note issued post year end
1918	76,343	received post year end
1478	94,871	MD has received assurances that will be paid - o/s from June
1451	38,321	we also have creditors balance with this company - will not pay until this is settled
	550,159	

Prepare the audit workpaper on debtors recoverability and bring any potential adjustments to audit adjustment schedule.

Task 2.5.4

You have a junior back in the office chasing up debtors circularisations and inputting the information onto a spreadsheet. The junior sends you the workpaper as it stands:

Steelx Limited **Debtors Circularisations**		prepared by reviewed by	PB	Date:
Customer	balance per ledger €/£	balance per debtors circ €/£		comment
1174	34,578	34,578		signed letter received
1047	69,487	34,978		statement received from customer of balance
1274	41,578			customer said that the signed confirmation was sent directly to Steelx Limited - to get from FD
1463	24,568			customer has signed but not noted whether agree or disagree
1765	68,478	68,478		signed letter received
1864	35,487			letter returned unopened - no company existed at this address. Cannot get contact number to phone
1687	15,487			contacted by phone - will send in as soon as possible
1879	10,847 300,510	10,847		signed letter received

You will now get Matthew to complete the audit work on the above worksheet – indicate the audit work you wish Matthew to carry out on the above results.

Section 2.6 Income Statement

Task 2.6.1

Louise asks you to review the analysis of expenses she received from Paula. Following review, she has asked you to draft a memorandum indicating what further work should be performed on the analytical review of operating expenses.

Review of operating expenses

	2007 €/£	2006 €/£	Comments
Insurance	24,987	12,487	increase in premium
Salaries	476,152	402,678	increase in staff numbers by 2; plus recruitment costs in relation to hire of credit controller
Distribution costs	245,781	124,687	some included in cost of sales in prior year
Repairs and maintenance	78,654	24,687	significant improvements made to reception area
Computer costs	14,567	12,457	
Audit fees	21,487	14,578	saville and sonner fees
Rent and rates	14,578	10,248	increase in rate charges
	876,206	601,822	

Task 2.6.2

Matthew overhears Louise and yourself talking about the profit and loss variances. He asks you to explain to him why you have chosen to use analytical procedures when auditing the profit and loss account. Furthermore, he is confused when he hears you talking about further substantive work being required. Explain to Matthew the use of analytical procedures and indicate the circumstances where further substantive work may be needed.

Task 2.6.3

Mark has come to you in relation to the wages reconciliation. He states that Paula is going to reconcile them for you, however, it is not clear from the planning list exactly what they should be reconciling. He asks you to send Paula an e-mail explaining exactly what sort of wages reconciliation you require. He asks you to be very detailed in your explanation and request as Paula is under pressure.

Prepare the e-mail to send to the client in relation to requirements for a wages reconciliation.

Section 2.7   Completion

You have now completed all the fieldwork on site and have arrived back in the office. Louise is finishing up the file to give to John for partner review. Louise has asked you to do a completion memorandum for the file on the work that you have carried out. This can be then issued to the partner for subsequent discussion and agreement with the client. The memo should contain the following:

- Issues which arose from your sections
- A list of all potential audit adjustments
- Any management recommendations

SESSION THREE
THE IMPACT OF THE AUDIT AND ASSURANCE WORK ON THE CONTENT OF THE AUDIT REPORT ISSUED AT THE CONCLUSION OF THE AUDIT/ASSURANCE PROCESS

THE IMPACT OF THE AUDIT AND ASSURANCE WORK ON THE CONTENT OF THE AUDIT REPORT ISSUED AT THE CONCLUSION OF THE AUDIT/ASSURANCE PROCESS

Learning Outcome:

At the end of this session you should be able to have an understanding and appreciation of the following:

- The principles underpinning audit reporting
- Matters that do not affect the auditors opinion
- Matters that do affect the auditors opinion
- Most likely circumstances where, in practice, audit reports may need to be modified/qualified

Competency Level Expected – U and A

Required Reading:

Cosserat – Chapter 17

CAP 2 (ICAI) Auditing Manual Relevant Chapters

ISA (UK & Ireland) 700: The Auditor's Report on Financial Statements

Before you get started, answer the short-form questions overleaf. These will help you to familiarise yourself with the topic!

> **Short Form Questions**
>
> 1. Give two examples of situations where it is appropriate for an auditor to issue an adverse audit opinion
> 2. What would be the effect on an audit report opinion if there was a disagreement between the directors and the auditor with regard to the accounting treatment or disclosures of matters in the financial statements?
> 3. Set out briefly your understanding of the terms "inherent uncertainty" and "fundamental uncertainty". Your answer should include an illustrative example
> 4. State four matters that an auditor should consider immediately prior to physically signing the audit report

Task 3.1

John has reviewed the file and has a close out meeting scheduled with the client tomorrow. He is concerned that Mark will be shocked at the number of audit adjustments as he was expecting very few.

John has asked you to do a memo for the client of all the issues noted in the completion memo to John and the potential implications for the audit report if adjustments are not posted.

Audit Workbook

Suggested Solution

Section 2

Short Form Questions

1. Four from the following:

    - Establishing level of any type of risk (eg fraud, inherent, control, detection etc)
    - Whether any particular item is material/immaterial/fundamental
    - Whether a debt is recoverable/doubtful/bad
    - The adequacy of any provision/level of claim likely to arise from litigation
    - The useful lives of assets (tangible or intangible)
    - Whether the accounts as a whole give a true and fair view
    - Whether an entity is likely to be a going concern
    - Income recognition for software sales
    - Deferral of costs
    - Recognition of profit/foreseeable losses on long term contract work in progress
    - Whether a transaction or accounting policy complies with company law/accounting standards

2. Alternative procedures

    - Resend confirmation letter: 2nd and 3rd follow up letters
    - Telephone/fax enquiry – with check that fax has been sourced directly from debtor
    - Subsequent cash with inspection of customer's remittance advice
    - Review invoices/delivery notes making up the balance

3. The following are the key procedures that an auditor should undertake during a stocktake:

    - Ascertain whether the client's staff are carrying out their instructions properly so as to provide reasonable assurance that the stocktaking will be accurate
    - Carry out test counts to satisfy himself/herself that procedures and internal controls relating to the stocktaking are working

properly. If the manner of carrying out the stocktaking or the results of the test counts are not satisfactory, the auditor should immediately draw the matter to the attention of the management supervising the stocktaking and he/she may have to request a recount of part, or all of the stocks
- When carrying out test counts, the auditor should select items both from count records and from the physical stocks and should check one to the other to gain assurance as to the completeness and accuracy of the count records
- Pick stocks which have a high value either individually or as a category of stock
- Take photocopies of (or extracts from) rough stock sheets and details of the sequence of stock sheets
- Determine whether the procedures for identifying damaged, obsolete and slow moving stock operate properly. The auditor should obtain, from observations and by discussion, information about the stocks' condition, age, usage and, in the case of work in progress, its stage of completion
- Ensure no third party stock included or client stock at third party premises omitted
- The auditor should consider whether management has instituted adequate cut-off procedures, i.e. procedures intended to ensure that movements into, within and out of stocks are properly identified and reflected in the accounting records

4. Four of the following:

- Quantify the total petty cash spend in the year
- Determine if this casts doubts on the reliability of the financial controller and the effect this has on other aspects of the audit
- Increase the substantive testing on petty cash and analyse the categories of cash expenditure
- Establish who in the company was aware of this procedure
- If, after reviewing the matter, you suspect a fraud is being perpetrated:
    - communicate your findings to the appropriate level of management, the board of directors or the audit committee

- If the suspected fraud casts doubt on the integrity of the directors we should make a report to ODCE without informing the directors in advance

• If you determine a fraud may have occurred then it should be reported to the Garda Siochana as required under the Criminal Justice (Fraud and Offences) Act 2001.

5. Tests of control procedures that an auditor may adopt in obtaining evidence about the effective operation of internal controls over fixed assets include:

   • Random sample check of the fixed asset register to ensure proper updating and recording of acquisitions and disposals
   • Compare actual capital expenditure on fixed assets with budgeted expenditure and seek explanations for any major deviations
   • Investigate and enquire as to how budgeted expenditure is monitored on an ongoing basis
   • Enquire and document the procedures for ensuring delivery and inspection of assets prior to payment
   • Observe the security procedures in place to safeguard the assets, eg security personnel used, locking of premises at close of business etc
   • Inspect minutes of meetings for evidence of management review of capital expenditure, budgets and other internal control procedures in place
   • Document the procedure for updating the fixed asset register and carry out a 'walk-through' test to ensure the system is working properly
   • Review the documented results of any work on internal controls of fixed assets, performed by the internal auditors

6. The reliability of audit evidence is influenced by its source: internal and external, and by its nature: visual, documentary or oral. While the reliability of audit evidence is dependent on individual circumstance, the following generalisations may help in assessing that reliability:

   • Audit evidence from external sources (for example confirmation received from a third party) is more reliable than that obtained from the entity's records

- Audit evidence obtained from the entity's records is more reliable when the related accounting and internal control system operates effectively
- Evidence obtained directly by auditors is more reliable than that obtained by or from the entity
- Evidence in the form of documents and written representations is more reliable than oral representations
- Original documents are more reliable than photocopies or facsimiles

7. The steps normally involved in the review and testing of the process used by management or the directors are:

- Evaluation of the data and consideration of the assumptions on which the estimate is based
- Testing of the calculations involved in the estimate
- Comparison, when possible, of estimates made for prior periods with actual results of those periods
- Consideration of management's or the directors' review and approval procedures

8. The following are the quality control procedures that an auditor may adopt:

- Professional requirements – policies to ensure personnel adhere to the principles of independence, integrity, objectivity, confidentiality and professional behaviour
- Skills and competence – policies to ensure personnel have attained and maintain the technical standards and professional competence required to enable them to fulfill their responsibilities with due care
- Acceptance and retention of clients – prospective clients are evaluated and existing clients are reviewed on an ongoing basis. In making a decision to accept or retain a client, the auditors independence and ability to serve the client properly and the integrity of the client's management are considered
- Assignment – audit work is assigned to personnel who have the degree of technical training and proficiency required in the circumstances

- Delegation (direction, supervision and review) – sufficient direction, supervision and review of work at all levels is carried out in order to provide confidence that the work performed meets appropriate standards of quality
- Consultation – consultation, whenever necessary, within or outside the audit firm occurs with those who have appropriate expertise
- Monitoring – the continued adequacy and operational effectiveness of quality control policies are monitored

9. When considering whether the accounting policies adopted by management are acceptable the auditor needs to have regard to:

    - Policies commonly adopted in particular industries
    - Policies for which there is substantial authoritative support
    - Whether departures from applicable accounting standards are necessary for the financial statements to give a true and fair view
    - Whether the financial statements reflect the substance of the underlying transactions and not merely their form

10. Existence:

    - Consider attending at third party premises at the time of the year-end stock count or subsequently
    - Obtain confirmation of stock existence in writing from the third party

    Valuation

    - Normal valuation procedures that an auditor would apply to non third party stocks would be relevant eg:
        - Ensure stock valued at lower of cost and net realisable value
        - Test check a sample of items to purchase invoices
        - Ensure amounts are properly totted
    - Ensure that valuation procedures include third party stocks

11. Procedures undertaken to ensure that the company maintains proper books of account:

    - Establish whether detailed records were kept for all revenues, expenses, journal entries and any other significant transactions

- Review relevant legislation and ensure that the company is in compliance with the legislative requirements (S202 of the 1990 Companies Act – ROI; S229 of he Companies (NI) Order 1990 – NI)
- Establish whether periodic management accounts were prepared during the year
- Determine the scale of adjustments required from the trial balance to the final draft accounts
- Determine whether there were any accounting breakdowns
- Determine whether there were any undue delays in processing transactions

12. The detailed Profit and Loss account does not form part of the audited financial statements and thus the auditor does not give any opinion on it. It therefore falls under remit of ISA (UK & Ireland) 720 Other Information in Documents Containing Audited Financial Statements. Accordingly the auditor should:

    - Read the information
    - Ensure it is consistent with the audited financial statements
    - Check accuracy of tots, categorizations etc
    - If the auditor becomes aware of any apparent misstatements therein, or identifies any material inconsistencies with the audited financial statements, they should seek to resolve them
    - If there is an issue, the auditor should raise it with the client and consider if it impacts on the audit opinion that will be given

13. Considerations in respect of the Audit of VAT

    - Ensure correct accounting procedures adopted, eg VAT not included within sales
    - Agree closing balance to back-up documentation
    - Check payment/receipt of the balance post period end
    - Agree a sample of payments/receipts in the year to the official receipts
    - Ensure VAT is up to date and returns were filed on a timely basis

- Ensure that any interest liability or penalties are provided for, if material
- Check correspondence in respect of any VAT inspections etc

14. The factors that must be considered in determining sample size are:
    - The level of risk the auditor is prepared to accept which would be determined by the auditors' assessment of the audit risk pertaining to a particular client
    - An acceptable error rate, which will depend on factors such as the quality of the internal controls etc
    - Population determination – stratification of the population and determining which strata to spend more time on due to its risk profile, thus lowering the sample size
    - The results of previous audit work will help in the analysis of the expected error rate

    The benefits of using statistical sampling are:
    - It is a sound scientific basis of choosing a sample using probability theory
    - It provides a uniform framework for making consistent judgments over time
    - It reduces personal bias in the choice of sample size and is thus more objective
    - The quality of the audit is improved as greater reliability can be placed on the results
    - It requires explicit consideration of all relevant factors

15. Completeness of sales and debtors:
    - Conduct a numerical sequence check on sales invoices to ensure that all sales are recorded
    - Review and vouch the debtors control account reconciliation to underlying books and records
    - Perform detailed cut-off testing
    - Carry out analytical procedures

Section 2.1

Materiality

Materiality can be based on % of profit before tax, revenue or total assets. The recommended materiality basis in Steelx Limited is profit before tax. However, since Steelx Limited is currently reporting a loss, revenue is a more suitable basis for materiality. Materiality for Steelx Limited can be calculated as follows:

Revenue	£/€15,425,063
Measurement %	.005
Planning materiality	74,744

Preliminary Analytical Review

On review of the trial balance presented to the auditors at the planning meeting, the following points should be noted:

- Revenue has increased by 9% whereas cost of sales has increased by 22%. This is likely to be as a direct result of rising steel prices, but this resultant drop in gross margin will be discussed with the client in detail
- Rent has decreased by £/€40k from the prior year – will need to ensure that all costs have been included in correct period
- Repairs and maintenance has increased by €/£54k – this will be reviewed for any capital items
- Staff pension contributions have decreased by €/£87k – this may be due to a once off payment in prior year, or indeed an under-accrual in the current year. This will be investigated in details
- Distribution costs have increased by €/£120k (50%) when revenue has only increased by 9% – analysis of this code will be obtained and reviewed in detail to ensure costs have been posted correctly
- There is provision for doubtful debts in the current year where there was none in prior year. Discussions will be held with management as to the requirement for the provision in the current year – has there been any developments with customers that suggest they will not be in a position to pay their debt
- Corporation tax charge has yet to be posted

- There are significant plant and motor vehicle additions during the year – these will be traced to invoices for verification
- Stock has decreased during the year which was not expected given the increase in purchases – this will be investigated
- Prepayments have increased by over 50% from the prior year – this will be reviewed to ensure cut-off is treated correctly
- Accruals have increased by €/£73k – these will be reviewed to ensure cut-off treated correctly

Significant Areas
On review of the trial balance and planning meeting minutes, the critical areas are as follows:

Stock
Stock has been identified as a significant area due to risk level on the basis that there was an adjustment between system and physical stock at the year end.

Creditors and accruals
Accruals has been identified as a significant area due to large number of accruals which are based on client estimates. Existence and valuation are critical.

Wages and Salaries
Due to difficulties noted during the planning meeting, this area is regarded as critical – valuation and cut-off are significant areas.

Section 2.2

Task 2.2.1

FIXED ASSET WORK PROGRAMME

Client: Steelx Limited
Year Ended: 31 December 2007

Prepared By: JC
Reviewed By: LK
Date: 17 March 2008

Procedue	Reference
1. Cast the fixed asset subsidiary ledgers and agree the total with the general ledger accounts. Prepared a fixed asset lead schedule.	See **E1**
2. Scan the repairs and maintenance account items for reasonableness, noting any large or unusual items.	See **E300**
3. Obtain, prepare or update a permanent file schedule summarising the fixed asset capitalisation policies and review for appropriateness and consistency of accounting method with the prior year.	See **E350**
4. Identify significant fixed assets additions: a) Examine appropriate supporting documents. b) Ensure that VAT has been accounted for properly. c) Ensure additions have been recorded correctly.	See **E400**
5. Review all material disposals of assets and examine appropriate supporting documents. Ensure that the profit / loss on disposal are calculated correctly and disposal is recorded correctly.	See **E450**
6. Determine whether depreciation or amortisation charged to profit and loss account is calculated on a consistent and reasonable basis.	See **E600**

Client: Steelx Limited E1

Year Ended: 31-Dec-07 **Prepared By:** JC
Subject: Fixed Asset Lead Schedule **Reviewed By:** LC

		Computer Equipment	Motor Vehicles	Plant & Machinery	Total	
COST						
Opening balance		20,743	127,352	312,604	460,699	✗
					Ω	
Additions	(E400)	3,484	85,483	131,809	220,776	✗
					Ω	
Disposals	(E450)	0	(23,787)	0	(23,787)	✗
					Ω	
Closing balance		24,227	189,048	444,413	657,688	✗
		Ω	Ω	Ω	Ω	
ACCUMULATED DEPRECIATION						
Opening balance		(20,445)	(55,086)	(174,776)	(250,307)	✗
					Ω	
Charge for year	(E600)	(1,850)	(52,393)	(35,771)	(90,014)	✗
					Ω	
Depreciation on disposals		0	21,804	0	21,804	✗
					Ω	
Closing balance		(22,295)	(85,675)	(210,547)	(318,517)	✗
		Ω	Ω	Ω	Ω	
NBV						
As at 31 December 2007		1,932	103,373	233,866	339,171	✗
		Ω	Ω	Ω	Ω	
As at 31 December 2006		298	72,266	137,828	210,392	✗
		Ω	Ω	Ω	Ω	

AUDIT TICKS

✗ Agrees to client fixed asset register filed at **E2**.

Ω Tots checked and correct

Client: Steelx Limited
Year Ended: 31-Dec-07
Subject: Depreciation

E2

Prepared By: JC
Reviewed By: LC

Asset Code	Description	Date of addition/ disposal	Life	Opening Cost	Additions/ (Disposals)	Closing Cost	Opening Dep	YTD Depn	Disposal	Closing Depn	NBV	Audit Dep Check	Audit Diff
COMPUTER EQUIPMENT													
821	Server			19,876		19,876	19,876			19,876	–	–	
859	SCANNER/SOFTWARE	01/06/2007	2		3,484	3,484		1,742		1,742	1,742	1,016	726
778	/KEYBOARD/MONITOR		8	867		867	569	108		677	190	108	0
Total				20,743	3,484	24,227	20,445	1,850		22,295	1,932	1,125	726
MOTOR VEHICLES													
834	HYUNDAI SONATA		2	17,089		17,089	8,545	8,545		17,089	–	8,544	0
920	FORD FOCUS VAN	01/10/2007	4		11,983	11,983	0	749		749	11,234	749	0
832	BMW 528i		2	21,775		21,775	10,888	10,887		21,775	–	10,888	(0)
833	VOLVO	01/11/2007	2	13,473	(13,473)	0	6,736	5,614	(12,350)	0	–	5,614	0

Client:	Steelx Limited													E2
Year Ended:	31-Dec-07													Prepared By: JC
Subject:	Depreciation													Reviewed By: LC

Asset Code	Description	Date of addition/ disposal	Life	Opening Cost	Additions/ (Disposals)	Closing Cost	Opening Dep	YTD Depn	Disposal	Closing Depn	NBV	Audit Dep Check	Audit Diff
835	VOLVO	01/11/2007	2	10,314	(10,314)	0	5,157	4,298	(9,455)	0	–	4,298	0
836	BMW 325i		4	64,703	0	64,703	23,761	16,176		39,937	24,766	16,176	0
888	TOYOTA AVENIS	01/09/2007	4		24,500	24,500		2,042		2,042	22,458	2,042	0
889	TOYOTA AVENIS	01/09/2007	4		24,500	24,500		2,042		2,042	22,458	2,042	0
890	MAZDA	10/01/2008	4		24,500	24,500		2,042		2,042	22,458	0	2,042
Total				127,354	61,696	189,050	55,087	52,395	(21,805)	85,676	103,374	50,353	2,042

62 AUDITING AND ASSURANCE TOOLKIT

Asset Code	Description	Date of addition/ disposal	Life	Opening Cost	Additions/ (Disposals)	Closing Cost	Opening Dep	YTD Depn	Closing Depn	NBV	Audit Dep Check	Audit Difference
PLANT & MACHINERY												
858	WAREHOUSE RACKING	02/02/2007	8		9,659	9,659	–	1,207	1,207	8,452	1,107	101
860	COMBILIFT FORKLIFT S/N 8483	01/08/2007	5		47,100	47,100	–	9,420	9,420	37,680	3,925 -	5,495
740	SHELVING		8	6,819		6,819	2,879	492	3,371	3,447	852 -	360
757	OFFICE FURNITURE		8	28,502		28,502	17,873	1,329	19,202	9,300	3,563 -	2,234
758	PHONE SYSTEM		8	4,190		4,190	1,287	363	1,650	2,540	524 -	161
768	CHANNELLS FOR MATERIAL STORAGE		8	6,399		6,399	4,276	265	4,541	1,857	800 -	535
770	CONF. ROOM FURNITURE		8	2,506		2,506	1,200	163	1,363	1,143	313 -	150
775	FORK LIFT RAMP		8	6,031		6,031	2,761	409	3,170	2,861	754 -	345
783	PAINTING OF RACKING		8	18,720		18,720	14,233	561	14,794	3,926	2,340 -	1,779
790	BEAM SAW AP		5	41,062		41,062	5,128	7,187	12,315	28,747	8,212 -	1,026
810	CANON IR2010F FAX MACHINE		5	3,000		3,000	1,654	269	1,923	1,077	600 -	331
746	CARPETS NEW BUILDING		8	14,360		14,360	8,374	748	9,122	5,238	1,795 -	1,047
747	ELECTRICAL FITTINGS		8	25,490		25,490	19,082	801	19,883	5,607	3,186 -	2,385
750	LEASEHOLD IMPROVEMENTS		12	82,578		82,578	64,234	1,529	65,763	16,816	6,882 -	5,353
752	LEGAL FEES ASSET 5750		8	3,054		3,054	1,267	223	1,490	1,563	382 -	158
756	WIRING/ DATA POINTS		8	11,428		11,428	5,679	719	6,398	5,030	1,428 -	710
759	BLINDS (ALL OFFICES)		8	1,016		1,016	543	59	602	414	127 -	68

IMPACT OF AUDIT AND ASSURANCE WORK ON THE CONTENT OF THE AUDIT REPORT 63

No.	Description	Date	Life									
763	ALARM SYSTEM		8	8,215		8,215	4,212	500	4,712	3,503	1,027 -	527
794	ELECTRICAL WORK		8	6,392		6,392	2,091	538	2,629	3,763	799 -	261
795	ELECTRICAL WORK		8	1,181		1,181	789	49	838	343	148 -	99
799	ADD CABLING & DATA POINTS		8	2,502		2,502	1,298	150	1,448	1,053	313 -	162
801	STAIRS TO ROOF AREA		8	3,275		3,275	1,290	248	1,538	1,737	409 -	161
802	LIFTING TABLE FOR ROOF AREA		8	1,250		1,250	374	110	484	767	156 -	47
806	ELECTRICAL WORK (WAREHOUSE)		8	1,210		1,210	289	115	404	806	151 -	36
807	ELECTRICAL WORK (WAREHOUSE)		8	1,414		1,414	309	138	447	967	177 -	39
782	MATERIALS & MOVEMENT FLT BATT		8	4,000		4,000	1,709	286	1,995	2,005	500 -	214
784	FORKLIFT PARTS		8	5,700		5,700	2,767	367	3,134	2,567	713 -	346
789	FORKLIFT TRUCK AP		3	6,266		6,266	2,398	1,289	3,687	2,579	2,089 -	799
812	JUNGHEINRICH FLT OVERHAUL		5	7,543		7,543	4,390	631	5,021	2,523	1,509 -	878
813	80V BATTERIES CESAB SDTRACKER		5	8,500		8,500	2,390	1,222	3,612	4,888	1,700 -	478
861	COMBILIFT FORKLIFT	01/02/2007	5		71,500	71,500		14,300	14,300	57,200	13,108	1,192
919	FORK LIFT 48V BATTERY	01/01/2007	5		3,550	3,550		710	710	2,840	710	
	Total			312,603	131,809	444,412	174,776	46,397	221,173	223,239	60,298 -	13,900
	Grand Total			460,699	136,746	597,446	195,221	90,014	232,842	179,039	111,773 -	11,132

Client:	Steelx Limited		**E300**
Year Ended:	31-Dec-07	**Prepared By:**	JC
Subject:	Repairs and Maintenance Review	**Reviewed By:**	LC
		Date:	18/03/2008

Objective: To ensure no large or unusual items are included in the repairs and maintenance nominal ledger that would require adjustment

Procedure: Review the repairs and maintenance nominal accounts for reasonableness, noting any large or unusual items

Result: The repairs and maintenance summary has been reviewed for reasonableness. On review, the following invoices were noted as being capital items:

	€/£
JK Office fitters	13,768
Furniture for you	17,980
	31,748

These relate to the refurbishment of the reception area.

These should be included in fixed asset additions and depreciated - the following adjustment has been brought to the Audit Adjustment Schedule:

		€/£	€/£
DR	Plant and machinery additions	31,748	
CR	Repairs and maintenance		31,748

being correction of capital items included in repairs and maintenance

		€/£	€/£
DR	Depreciation charge	3,307	
CR	Accumulated depreciation		3,307

being depreciation of assets from date of acquisition. See workings below.

Depreciation Calculation

	€/£	
JK Office fitters	13,768	acquired 23/02/08 – 10 months depreciation
Furniture for you	17,980	acquired 03/03/08 – 10 months depreciation
	31,748	
depreciation for one year	3,969	8 year UEL in line with other assets on FAR
depreciation for 10 months	3,307	

Conclusion: Fixed assets have been incorrectly included in repairs and maintenance. The proposed adjustments are material and should be discussed with the client and posted. All adjustments have been brought to Audit Adjustment Schedule.

Client:	Steelx Limited		E350
Year Ended:	31-Dec-07	**Prepared By:**	JC
Subject:	Capitalisation Policy	**Reviewed By:**	LC
		Date:	18/03/2008

Objective: To ensure capitalisation policy is appropriate and consistent

Procedure: Review the capitalisation policy for appropriateness and consistency of accounting method with the prior year

Result: As discussed with management in the planning meeting, there is no fixed capitalisation policy. The MD reviews all invoices and indicates which should be capitalised. This method has led to errors since per **E300**, capital items were included in the repairs and maintenance nominal.

To avoid these errors and to adopt best practice, the company should implement a capitalisation policy. This has been brought to the Management Recommendations.

Conclusion: No fixed asset capitalisation policy exists - this has been brought to the Management Recommendations.

Client:	Steelx Limited		**E400**
Year Ended:	31-Dec-07	**Prepared By:**	JC
Subject:	Fixed Asset Additions	**Reviewed By:**	LC
		Date:	18/03/2008

Objective: To ensure significant additions have been recorded correctly

Procedure: Review significant additions:
- examine appropriate supporting documentation
- ensure vat has been properly accounted for
- ensure recorded correctly

Result: Fixed asset additions are summarised as follows:

COMPUTER EQUIPMENT

€/£

01/06/2007 Scanner/software   E1   3,484   *not material - no further work required*

E1

MOTOR VEHICLES

€/£

Date	Item		Amount	Ref
01/10/2007	Ford Focus Van		11,983	**(E401)**
01/09/2007	Toyota Avensis		24,500	**(E402)**
01/09/2007	Toyota Avensis		24,500	**(E402)**
10/01/2008	Mazda 6	note	24,500	**(E403)**
		E1	85,483	(continued)

PLANT & MACHINERY

	€/£	
Warehouse Racking	9,659	*not material - no further work required*
Combilift Forklift	47,100	**(E404)**
Combilift Forklift	71,500	**(E405)**
Forklift Battery	3,550	*not material - no further work required*

E1 | **131,809**

Note

This asset should be recorded in subsequent year and as a result, the following adjustment has been brought to the Audit Adjustment Schedule:

		€/£	€/£
DR	Trade Creditors	29,645	
CR	Motor vehicle additions		24,500
CR	VAT		5,145

being correction of motor vehicle recorded in incorrect period

Conclusion: With the exception of additions not posted as per **E300**, and the note above fixed asset additions have been recorded correctly and traced to appropriate documentation.

Steelx Ltd.

Kylemore Industrial Estate

Dublin

E401

Mayday Motors

1 Main Street

Athlone

Co. Westmeath

Date: 01/10/2007

Invoice Number: 19873

Description	Quantity	Price
Ford Focus Van E400	1	£/€11,983
VAT at 21%		2,517
	Total	£/€14,500

VAT registration number: 425656

Steelx Ltd.
Kylemore Industrial Estate
Dublin

E402
Mayday Motors
1 Main Street
Athlone
Co. Westmeath

Date: 01/09/2007

Invoice Number: 19872

Description	Quantity	Price
Toyota Avensis E400	2	£/€49,000
VAT at 21%		10,290
	Total	£/€59,290

VAT registration number: 425656

Steelx Ltd.
Kylemore Industrial Estate
Dublin

E403
Mayday Motors
1 Main Street
Athlone
Co. Westmeath

Date: 10/01/2008

Invoice Number: 12356

Description	Quantity	Price
Mazda E400	1	£/€24,500.00
VAT at 21%		5,145
	Total	£/€29,645.00

VAT registration number: 425656

Steelx Ltd.

Kylemore Industrial Estate

Dublin

E404

Mayday Motors

1 Main Street

Athlone

Co. Westmeath

Date: 01/08/2007

Invoice Number: 17983

Description	Quantity	Price
Combilift Forklift S/N 8483 E400	1	£/€41,100.00
VAT at 21%		8,631
	Total	£/€49,731

VAT registration number: 425656

Steelx Ltd.

Kylemore Industrial Estate

Dublin

E405

Mayday Motors

1 Main Street

Athlone

Co. Westmeath

Date: 01/02/2007

Invoice Number: 17883

Description	Quantity	Price
Combilift Forklift S/N 8483 E400	1	£/€71,500.00
VAT at 21%		15,015
Total		£/€86,515.00

VAT registration number: 425656

Client:	Steelx Limited		E450
		Prepared By:	JC
Year Ended:	31-Dec-07	**Reviewed By:**	LC
Subject:	Fixed Asset Disposals	**Date:**	18/03/2008

Objective: To ensure significant disposals have been recorded correctly

Procedure: Review disposals and ensure profit/loss is correctly calculated. Ensure disposals are recorded correctly.

Result Fixed asset disposals are summarised as follows:

MOTOR VEHICLES

Asset	Cost	Acc Dep	NBV	Proceeds	(Profit)/Loss	
Volvo	13,473	(12,350)	1,123	3,000	(1,877)	
Volvo	10,314	(9,455)	859	3,000	(2,141)	
	23,787	(21,805)	1,982	6,000	(4,018)	↗
	⌢	⌢	⌢	⌢		

AUDIT TICKS

↗ Agreed to trial balance

⌢ Agreed to client fixed asset register as per E2

Conclusion: Fixed asset disposals have been recorded correctly

Client:	Steelx Limited		E600
Year Ended:	31-Dec-07	**Prepared By:**	JC
Subject:	Depreciation	**Reviewed By:**	LC
		Date:	18/03/2008

Objective: To ensure depreciation has been calculated and recorded correctly

Procedure: Review depreciation charged to the profit and loss account to determine if it has been calculated on a consistent and reasonable basis.

Result: Depreciation was checked on the fixed asset register on E2 and it was noted that depreciation was under-stated by £/€11,132. The following journal has been brought to Audit Adjustment Schedule:

			€/£	
DR	Depreciation charge profit and loss		11,132	
DR	Accumulated depreciation - computer equipment		726	
DR	Accumulated depreciation - motor vehicles		2,042	
CR	Accumulated depreciation - plant and machinery			13,900

being correction of depreciation charge

Conclusion: Depreciation charge has been calculated incorrectly and proposed adjustment has been brought to the Audit Adjustment Schedule.

Task 2.2.2

Additional tests which should be included in a fixed asset programme are as follows:

- Verify ownership of significant land and buildings
  - Confirm title deeds
- Verify the physical existence of significant assets
  - Physically inspect sample of assets
- Enquire whether all new and existing lease agreements are identified and properly accounted for (obtain copies of leases and other continuing data for inclusion in the permanent file) and update our permanent file schedules
  - Ask client if any new lease agreements
  - If so reconcile lease agreement to closing liability and interest charge
  - Check bank for potential lease payments
- Enquire whether any fixed assets have been pledged as security
  - Ask client and confirm by bank confirmation
- Confirm that there is adequate insurance cover in place in respect of all fixed assets
  - Review payments for insurance
  - Trace to insurance policy and schedule

Section 2.3

Task 2.3.1

Note 1

- Check dispatch note dated before stock count
- Trace goods received note before the year end to verify stock returned
- Ensure sale has been credited and is not included in current year stock

Note 2

- Get listing of stock held at third party
- Get third party confirmation
- Consider if physical verification is necessary

Note 3

- Trace original order, invoice and dispatch note
- Trace communication from customer indicating incorrect quantity
- Check goods receipt note and subsequent credit note to customer
- Trace to provision in ledger
- Physically inspect stock and discuss management intentions for this stock – ensure it does not have a scrap value

Note 4

- Trace order dated after the year end
- Check invoice dated after the year end – ensure recorded in correct period
- Check goods dispatch note
- Review procedure for picking stock and setting aside prior to dispatch to ensure in line with management representations and procedures

Note 5

- Count stock item at date of audit fieldwork and carry out roll-back procedures to get correct count of stock at year end

Task 2.3.2

MEMORANDUM

TO: Matthew Murphy
FROM: Louise Clarke
SUBJECT: Stock Count Sample
DATE: X/X/XX

ISA (UK and Ireland) 501 paragraph 5 states that 'When inventory is material to the financial statements, the auditor should obtain sufficient appropriate audit evidence regarding its existence and condition by attendance at physical inventory counting unless impracticable'

The auditor should attend the stock count and in line with ISA (UK & Ireland) 501, design procedures to confirm whether management:

- Maintains adequate inventory records that are kept up-to-date
- Has satisfactory procedures for inventory counting and test-counting

- Investigates and corrects all material differences between the book inventory records and the physical counts.

The auditor attends a physical inventory count to gain assurance that the inventory checking as a whole is effective in confirming that accurate inventory records are maintained. If the entity's inventory records are not reliable the auditor may need to request management to perform alternative procedures which may include a full count at the year end.

This memo deals with the 'test-counting' element of the stock take attendance. Various methods of sampling can be used to choose the sample, the most commonly used being the selection of high value items, as an error within these high value items could be material. This tests the existence of the items recorded on the rough stock sheets by the client, known as 'sheet to floor' count. However, with this method alone, there is a risk of stock being overstated since the audit team has not verified if stock sitting in the warehouse is included on the stock sheets. Therefore, in order to further test existence and valuation, a sample of stock items are selected from the warehouse floor and traced to the stock listing, known as 'floor to sheet' count.

Any discrepancies should be followed up with management and resolved prior to leaving the stock count.

Task 2.3.3

Client:	Prepared by:	Date:	Ref:
Year/Period End:	Reviewed by:	Date:	

STOCKTAKE ATTENDANCE WORK PROGRAMME - DRAFT

	General	*Schedule Reference or comment*	*Initials and Date*
1 (a)	Obtain and review the clients written procedures for counting, recording and valuing stock;		
(b)	Obtain names, titles and responsibilities of client staff assigned to stock counting;		
(c)	Determine sample size range before attending stocktake by gaining an estimate from the client of the stock value and discussing with Manager or In Charge Accountant (a minimum of 20 floor to sheet and 20 sheet to floor is required, but this will increase dependent on the stock value).		
2	Record the following details for each location visited:		
(a)	location(s) being counted;		
(b)	date(s) of count and attendance;		
(c)	types of stock held at location;		
(d)	approximate value of stock by category at location;		
(e)	details of any stocks at locations not covered by the count and any alternative method used to verify their existence (e.g. stocks held on behalf of the company by third parties. Gain written confirmation from the third party of such stocks);		

	(f)	Names, titles and responsibilities of client staff assigned to stock counting;		
	(g)	names of audit staff taking part.		
		Stock Counting		
3		Ascertain and note whether:		
	(a)	the stocktake teams were properly briefed prior to commencing the count;		
	(b)	the teams include people who are not responsible for the storing and recording of stock and work in progress;		
	(c)	stock was counted by teams of two (one counting and one checking and recording);		
	(d)	the teams were asked to identify and note damaged, slow moving or obsolete stock;		
	(e)	the teams were made aware of any stocks held on behalf of third parties and these were excluded from the count.		
4		Establish the high value stock items and ensure maximum coverage in the stock count.		
5		Determine whether:		
	(a)	the teams were counting and recording accurately;		
	(b)	the counts were being controlled to ensure that all stock was counted only once;		
	(c)	there was adequate control over stock sheets to ensure that they were all accounted for (e.g. pre-numbered).		

6	Where serially numbered sheets are used, record the numbers of all sheets used at the end of the count.		
7	Select a sample of items from completed stock sheets and check to ensure that the number has been recorded properly. (These should be followed through to final stock sheets at the final audit.)		
8	Count a sample of stock items from the floor and ensure that they have been recorded properly on the final stock sheets.		
9	If errors are found when conducting the sample checks, consider extending the original sample.		
	Ascertain whether the errors are:		
(a)	isolated incidents; or		
(b)	only evident within a particular stock range; or		
(c)	over the whole stock population.		
	Consider whether a partial or full stock re-count is necessary, and advise Manager or In Charge Accountant (if practical) before notifying client.		
10	Copy or extract details of a sample of rough stock sheets for checking at the final audit.		

11	Where stocks are valued at selling price less mark-up, record the shelf price of a number of stock items (a minimum of 10 would normally be required, but may increase or decrease dependent on the stock value).		
12	Ascertain whether any stock is held on behalf of a third party. Where applicable ensure that it has been separately identified and excluded from the count.		
13	Ascertain whether any consignment stock is held. Ensure, where appropriate, a full record is made.		
14	Note any old or damaged stock during the count. Ensure that it is marked as such on the final stock sheets.		
	Cut-off		
15	Ensure that no movements in or out took place during the stocktake.		
16	Record details of the last goods despatch numbers and the last goods received note numbers to follow up at the final audit		
	Other Work		
17	Perform any other procedures that would normally be carried out at the stocktake attendance, such as physical inspection of fixed assets and/or cash counts.		

	Conclusion		
18	Write a report on the stocktake, as soon as possible after the attendance, on its accuracy and the ability to rely on it and submit for review to Manager.		

Task 2.3.4

Background

Stock pricing tests involve verifying that stock has been valued at the lower of cost or net realisable value in line with the requirements of IAS 2, Inventories. This involves two elements of testing:

- Verifying cost
- Verifying net realisable value

Verifying stock cost

- For merchandise stock and raw materials valued in a first-in first-out (FIFO) basis, examine most recent suppliers invoices covering the quantity in stock
- For work-in-progress and finished goods stock, cost must be tested against costing records. This will involve tests of control over the process and auditors then vouch the costs that are applied to physical stock to the costing record

Verifying net realisable value

To verify the sales price of the stock, auditors must review the selling price of the product after the year end. If the product has not been sold at time of fieldwork, additional work must be carried out to substantiate the sales price. This may involve:

- Review and test pricing process set by management
- Use an independent estimate
- Market trends

Test Instructions

- Use statistical sampling to extract a sample for testing
- Verify cost by tracing to most recent supplier invoices

- For steel that was amended prior to sale, review and document clients procedures for valuing the stock, including any overheads. Review for reasonableness and trace costs to invoices
- For stock items sampled above, trace to sales invoices after the year end and note sales price on workpaper
- For items that were not sold post year end:
  - Discuss with management if stock is obsolete
  - Review potential for reduction in sales price
  - Consider the use of an expert to review sales price
- Conclude on items tested if stock is valued at lower of cost and net realisable value

Section 2.4

Task 2.4.1

Audit Accrual

- Agree to quote from partner

Employer liability insurance

- Trace to invoice
- It should be noted that the policy states that the employer is liable to a £/€50k excess but no accrual has been made. It was noted in the planning minutes that there were two accidents on site during the year for which claims have yet to be settled. It would be prudent at this stage to accrue for the £/€50k excess. This has been brought to Audit Adjustment Schedule for discussion with management:

DR	Insurance claim	50,000	
CR	Accruals		50,000

Being provision for employers liability excess

Rebate accrual

- Get details of agreed rates from management – discuss how these rates originated; check to customer correspondence if available
- Recalculate the rebates using the agreed rates for accuracy
- Review prior year rebate accrual and determine if any payments have been made during the year

- If no rebate payments have been made, consider reducing rebate accrual
- Consider sending confirmations if management refuse, consider implications for audit report, except for limitation of scope, if material balance.

Bonus accrual

- Review management calculations for bonus accrual
- Trace to post year end payment
- If bonus not yet paid, compare with prior year accrual and expectations

Goods received not invoiced

- Trace to goods received notes and ensure recorded in correct period
- Trace to post year end invoices
- Trace invoices as reconciling items on creditors reconciliation

Factory repairs

- Since factory repairs did not commence until 2008, accrual should not be included in current year
- Reversal of accrual has been brought to Audit Adjustment Schedule:

    DR   Accruals   15,000
    CR   Repairs and maintenance   15,000

    Being reversal of repairs accrual since they did not commence until after the year end

Task 2.4.2

Creditors reconciliations are required in order to verify the supplier balance included in the financial statements at the year end. There is a risk that the client may have understated liabilities and therefore creditors' reconciliations are used to satisfy the following audit assertions:

- Existence – confirmation of the balance directly from the supplier confirms that the liability exists
- Completeness – confirmation of the balance directly from the supplier confirms that all liabilities have been included

- Valuation – confirmation of the balance directly from the supplier confirms the value of the liability included in the financial statements

Therefore, creditors' reconciliation forms a very important part of the audit of creditors.

In most cases, supplier statements are included in the clients files, however, auditors must ensure that the statements are the original copies and have not been altered. Photocopied and faxed statements should not be relied upon, and if necessary, a copy should be requested directly from the supplier.

In selecting the sample of creditors' reconciliations to be tested, the sample should be chosen based on volume of purchases throughput, rather than year end balance, since the primary concern is that the recorded balance may be understated.

A creditors' reconciliation will reconcile the balance as per the supplier statement and the balance per the client ledger. Differences may arise where:

- Supplier sent invoice on last day of the year and is therefore included in supplier statement but has not been posted to client ledger. In this case, there should be a reconciling accrual if the goods have been received before the year end. The goods should be traced to goods received note before the year end and accrual should be traced to invoice received post year-end
- Payment made by client before the year end but did not reach the supplier until after the year end and as a result, the supplier statement does not include this payment. Payment should be traced to bank account before the year end
- Invoices which are in dispute may not have been posted by the client but included in supplier statement. Discuss with client reasons for not posting and consider potential accrual
- Credit note issued by supplier before the year end but not received by client until after the year end. Trace to credit note received after the year end.

Task 2.4.3

- Trace balance per supplier statement to original copy of statement. If a photocopy, consider requesting original directly from supplier
- Trace December payment of £/€7,800 to bank reconciliation and ensure recorded in correct period. Agree to subsequent month statement
- Agree invoices to goods received notes and ensure goods received before the year end
- Trace £/€44,507 to goods received not invoiced accrual
- Trace supplier balance to post year end payment if applicable

Task 2.4.4

For supplier balances with no supplier statements, the following audit work should be carried out:

- Trace all invoices and payments included in the supplier ledger activity for the period
- Agree the year end liability to invoices received after the year end
- Match the invoices to goods received notes and ensure goods received before the year end
- Trace year end liability to post year end payment
- Review post year end invoices to ensure no unrecorded liabilities

Section 2.5

Task 2.5.1

Steelx Limited

Audit Programme

Debtors and Prepayments

1. Test the addition of subsidiary ledgers (debtors, prepayments and accrued income) and agree the total with the general ledger control account. [completeness; existence]
2. Select a sample of credit notes and credit allowances:
   a. Examine credit notes and related documents for proper authorisation
   b. Determine whether the transaction dates are consistent with the period the transactions were recorded. [completeness]

3. Review sales and ensure that VAT/output tax is shown. Where no output tax is shown, ensure that this appears to be in accordance with VAT legislation. [completeness]

4. Ensure that the VAT treatment of credit notes is correct. [completeness]

5. Verify the appropriate cut-off of sales:
   a. Obtain last sales invoice number.
   b. Ascertain that the last sales invoice was included in the current year's recorded sales.
   c. Ascertain that the subsequent numbers are included in the subsequent year's recorded sales. [cut-off; completeness; existence]

6. Examine the sales records for at least the last seven days of the year.
   a. Select items to verify giving consideration to large or unusual entries in addition to "normal business" transactions.
   b. Verify that the selected items were recorded in the proper period by reference to shipping and other supporting documents.
   c. Verify that subsequent sales invoices are not included in current period revenues.
   d. Review production, dispatch notes, shipping and other supporting documents for at least the last seven days of the year to ensure all are included in current year recorded sales [cut-off; existence]

7. Examine the sales returns records for the period from the first business day of the next financial year through the current date.
   a. Select items to verify, giving consideration to large or unusual entries in addition to "normal business" transactions.
   b. Determine if selected items pertain to transactions that occurred before year-end and whether any adjustments are required. [cut-off; existence]

8. For sales where shipment has not occurred, review supporting documentation to verify appropriateness of accounting treatment and confirm such arrangements with the customer. [cut-off; existence]

9. Discuss large or unusual sales near year end with appropriate sales personnel. [cut-off; existence; completeness]

10. By sampling, confirm debtors, prepayments and accrued income balances or transactions by customer at or near year end, using positive confirmations.
    a. Determine sample size using statistical sampling.
    b. Select the sample for confirmation.
    c. Prepare confirmation requests and send via Sonner and Saville office
    d. Follow-up on accounts not confirmed at the client's request:
        1. List the accounts.
        2. Conduct alternative verification procedures eg verify to after date cash, or supporting documentation such as despatch notes, shipping documents, sales invoices and orders.
        3. Assess the effect on the scope of our examination and the content of our audit report.
    e. Investigate confirmation requests which are returned undelivered to determine whether the accounts are valid.
    f. Send second requests to non-responding customers.
    g. Consider sending third requests.
    h. For non-responding customers perform alternative audit procedures.
        1. Examine evidence of subsequent receipts clearly relating to the invoices which comprise balances or transactions in question.
        2. Examine customer orders or related correspondence or compare invoices to dispatch notes.
        3. Agree customer address to an independent source (e.g., telephone directory).
    i. If differences are reported on returned confirmations, document follow-up procedures and results.
        1. Report unresolved differences to appropriate client personnel.
        2. Determine whether such differences are caused by teeming and lading.
        3. Project sample results, and carry projected error, if any, to a Summary of Audit Differences.

11. Scan the revenue accounts in the general ledger for large or otherwise unusual entries:
    a. Large amounts recorded at or near year end.
    b. Large volume of transactions at or near year end.
    c. Unusual posting sources.
    d. Large journal entries at or near year end.

12. Test the provision for doubtful debts by:
    a. Test the ageing of the debtor records:
       1. Obtain an ageing by customer of debtor balances.
       2. Trace relevant documentation on sales and payment activity to verify that debtors have been properly aged.
    b. Identify customers that potentially pose a credit risk:
       1. Customers with significant over due accounts.
       2. Customers whose credit situation has declined during the year by comparing the ageing of debtors by significant customer to that existing at a previous period (e.g., last year).
       3. Customers where significant amounts were written off during the year.
    c. Review identified customers with appropriate client personnel.
    d. Review experience of recoveries of accounts previously written-off.
    e. Develop an estimate (or range) of the provision for doubtful debts and compare to the recorded provision.
    f. Discuss our estimate (or range) of the provision for doubtful debts with appropriate client personnel.
    g. Carry to the Summary of Audit Differences the difference, if any, between our estimate (or range) and the recorded amount.

13. Determine subsequent payment of over due accounts by examining remittance advices, bank deposit slips and bank statements. Consider having the client obtain independent credit reports and/or financial statements for customers with significant over due balances or balances in excess of credit limits.

Task 2.5.2

Review points on review of prepayments schedule:

- Include year end and date of audit work on workpaper
- Include prior period prepayments for comparison. Comment on any unusual variations form prior year
- Insert recalculation of rates prepayment; note that traced to original invoice; include period payment relates to; ensure enough information noted so work can be re-performed
- Obtain invoice for insurance prepayment and recalculate; include workings on workpaper
- List our miscellaneous prepayments and compare to prior period and expectations. Investigate any unusual items.

Task 2.5.3

				1460
Client:	Steelx Limited			
Year Ended:	31-Dec-07	Prepared By:	JC	
Subject:	Debtor recoverability	Reviewed By:	LC	
		Date:	20/03/2008	

Objective: To ensure year end debtors are recoverable

Procedure: Review debtors greater than 90 days for collectability. Compare with current bad debt provision and ensure it is adequate.

Results: The list of debtors greater than 90 days was received from the client and reviewed. From the comments received from the client, the following customer balances should be provided for:

Customer No	Balance	Potential Provision	Comment
1654	£/€ 65,487	£/€ 65,487	Since legal action is being taken to pursue payment on this balance, collectability is not guaranteed and therefore should be provided for
1687	164,587	164,587	This company has gone into liquidation and therefore payment of this debtor cannot be guaranteed - the full balance should therefore be provided
1248	49,876	49,876	This balance relates to a credit note raised after the year end. A provision should be made for this credit note in the current year
1478	94,871	47,436	Since this balance is greater than 6 months old, a provision should be considered. Though the MD has stated that payment has been promised, it would be prudent to provide for some of this balance - 50% provision has been brought to Audit Adjustment Schedule

Potential provision   327,386
Current provision   20,000
Increase required   307,386

An increase in the bad debt provision of £/€307,386 has been brought to the Schedule of Audit Adjustments:

    DR   Bad debt charge   307,386
    CR   Bad debt provision   307,386

Conclusion:
Trade debtors are overstated and should be reduced by the bad debt provision adjustment brought to the Schedule of Audit Adjustments

Task 2.5.4

1047

- Reconcile customer statement to balance on client ledger
- Trace all reconciling items to appropriate back-up and determine if valid
- Bring any potential adjustments to Schedule of Audit Differences

1274

No reliable audit evidence can be deducted from this reply since it was sent to the client. Therefore, additional audit work must be carried out:

- Examine correspondence filed with client
- Examine cash receipts post year end
- Examine goods dispatch notes to customer pre/post period end
- Consider additional circularization

1463

- Contact customer concerned and confirm whether balance agreed/disagreed
- If agreed, fax copy to client for signature and return
- If disagreed, obtain nature of disagreement and carry out further corroborative work in respect of disagreed items

1864

Confirm authenticity/accuracy of debtor balance by alternative means:

- Examine correspondence file with customer
- Examine order from customer
- Examination of telephone book
- Examination of trade journal
- Consider re-circularisation at new address

1687

- Continue to regularly follow up until received
- Note as outstanding point

Section 2.6

Task 2.6.1

Insurance

- Discuss with management reasons for increase in premiums
- Trace to invoices to ensure recorded in correct period
- Review insurance documentation/file to verify management explanations
- Consider if increase is consistent with current years trading results

Salaries

- Trace recruitment costs to invoices and transfer out of salaries
- Enquire from management the salaries of the new employees and use to calculate increase for reasonableness

Distribution costs

- Discuss with management disclosure between cost of sales and operating expenses
- Reanalyse prior year from cost of sales if necessary; or transfer portion in current year to be in line
- Test total distribution costs as a percentage of turnover and review for reasonableness
- Consider any financial reporting disclosure requirements

Rates

- Discuss reasons for increase with management. Review corroborative documentation
- Trace to invoices to ensure recorded in correct period

Task 2.6.2

Analytical procedures involve the use of comparisons of recorded accounting data with historical information, budget expectations, external benchmarks and/or industry/economic conditions. Analytical procedures enable the auditors to assess the overall reasonableness of account balances.

Analytical procedures can be used to replace substantive procedures where it is impractical to adopt fully substantive procedures. An example of this is the audit of operating expenses on an income statement. In large audits, it would not be practical to trace every invoice within certain expense categories to ensure its accuracy. Instead, expenses are reviewed and only those which do not meet with expectations are chosen for further substantive audit procedures.

The common types of analytical procedure involve a comparison of the entity's financial information with:

- Prior periods
- Expected results from budgets and forecasts
- Industry averages

Study the relevant Chapter of the audit text book for a detailed knowledge on analytical procedures.

Analytical procedures then allow the auditors to extract relationships which are unexpected. These are then discussed with management and if sufficient comfort has not been obtained, the auditor will perform further substantive testing to ensure accuracy of the financial statement amount. This may involve, for example, review of invoices and detailed analysis of expense codes. The use of analytical procedures in the audit of operating expenses therefore greatly reduces the audit work required.

Task 2.6.3

Wages reconciliations are used to reconcile the wages and salary figure in the financial statements to third party documentation. The third party documentation will take the form of gross to net listings, or a P35 which summarises total wages costs submitted to revenue for the year.

The gross to net listings/P35 will compute the total wages cost which is gross wages plus employers PRSI/NIC. However, this may not agree to the wages and salaries per the financial statements since also included in this figure may be health insurance, employee expenses, bonus accrual etc.

Therefore the wages reconciliation should be presented as follows:

Gross wages per gross to net	X
Employers PRSI/NIC	X
Total wages cost	X
Add reconciling items:	
Bonus accrual	X
Health insurance	X
Employee expenses	X
Salary accrual	X
Total wages and salaries per financial statements	X

It should be ensured that only costs relating to employees should be included in wages and salaries. For example, recruitment costs paid to a recruitment agency are not regarded as wages and salary costs.

Section 2.7

MEMORANDUM

TO: Audit File
FROM: James Crown
SUBJECT: Audit Findings

The audit work in Steelx Limited is now complete. Below is a summary of issues which arose in the audit of my sections.

Fixed Assets

- The repairs and maintenance nominal was reviewed for any capital items – it was noted that the costs in relation to the refurbishment of the reception area had been included as repairs and maintenance. Since these are adding to the value of the office, these have been brought to the Audit Adjustment Schedule for transfer to fixed asset additions. See adjustment 1.
- The fixed asset register was reviewed and depreciation calculations were checked for accuracy. As per E2, a number of the calculations

were incorrect and a correction adjustment has been brought to the Audit Adjustment Schedule – see adjustment 2.
- On reviewing additions, it was noted that a motor vehicle purchased on 10th January 2008 was included in current year additions. Since this was recorded in the incorrect period, an adjustment has been brought to Audit Adjustment Schedule to reverse – see adjustment 3.

Accruals

The schedule of accruals was audited and the following issues were noted:

- There was no accrual in relation to the outstanding employee claims for accidents on site. Though the insurance company will cover the claims, it states on the renewal invoice that the client is liable to an excess of £/€50,000. Since at this stage, it is not possible to compute the claims that will have to be paid to the employees, it is prudent to accrue for the excess. This adjustment has been brought to the Audit Adjustment Schedule – see adjustment 4.
- Additional work is required on the rebate accrual. At present, we have no substantive audit back-up to gain comfort over the rebate accrual. We need to do further testing on this balance, and will suggest confirmations to be sent to supplier to confirm balance.
- Included in accruals where factory repairs of £/€15,000, however these did not commence until after the year end. Since there was no evidence that these repairs had been contracted on before the year end, this accrual should be reversed and has been brought to the Audit Adjustment Schedule – see adjustment 5.

Debtors

The recoverability of debtors was reviewed by analysing all debtors greater than 90 days old. This highlighted substantial old debtors which did not appear to be recoverable and therefore should be provided. An increase in the bad debt provision has been brought to Audit Adjustment Schedule – adjustment 6.

See Audit Adjustment Schedule attached for details of all adjustments noted above.

Management Recommendations

During the audit fieldwork of the above sections, the following management recommendation was noted:

Weakness
There is no formal capitalisation policy. This can lead to inconsistencies and errors as in capitalization of expenses.

Recommendation
A formal policy should be implemented indicating that capital invoices over a set amount should automatically be capitalized. Furthermore, all invoices should be approved by the Financial Director to ensure policy is implemented.

Client: Steelx Limted
Year Ended: 31-Dec-07   **Prepared By:** JC
Subject: Audit Adjustment Schedule   **Reviewed By:** LC

	Detail of Adjustment	Actual Adjustments Dr/(Cr)	
		Balance Sheet	**Profit & Loss**
	Current Year Items:		
1	DR Fixed Asset Additions	31,748	
	CR Repairs and maintenance		(31,748)
	DR Depreciation charge		3,307
	CR Accumulated depreciation		

A2

being correction of capital items included in repairs and maintenance and depreciation thereof

2	DR Depreciation charge		3,307
	CR Accumulated depreciation	(3,307)	

being correction of depreciation charge on unrecorded assets

3	DR Trade Creditors	29,645	
	CR Motor Vehicle additions	(24,500)	
	CR VAT	(5,145)	

being correction of motor vehicle recorded in incorrect period

4	DR Insurance claims		50,000
	CR Accruals	(50,000)	

being provision of £/€50k excess re employers liability insurance

5	DR Accruals	15,000	
	CR Repairs and maintenance		(15,000)

being reversal of accrual since repairs did not commence until after the year end

6	DR Bad debt provision profit and loss		307,386
	CR Trade debtors	(307,386)	

being additional provision for debtors greater than 90 days

Section 3

Short Form Questions

1. An adverse opinion would be appropriate where the effect of a matter is fundamental to the financial statements and the auditor does not agree with the treatment of the matter. For example:

    - The preparation of accounts of a manufacturer in liquidation on a going concern basis without any adjustment
    - The inclusion of a non-existent asset in the financial statements that trebles the balance sheet size

2. According to ISA (UK & Ireland) 700 where the auditors disagree with the accounting treatment or disclosure of a matter in the financial statements:

    - The auditor should determine whether the effect of that disagreement is material to the financial statements
    - If it is material the auditor should include in the opinion section of their report
        i. A description of all substantive factors giving rise to the disagreement
        ii. Their implications for the financial statements
        iii. Whenever practicable a quantification of the effect on the financial statements
    - When the auditors conclude that the effect of the matter giving rise to disagreement is so material or pervasive that the financial statements are seriously misleading they should issue and adverse opinion
    - In the case of other material disagreements the auditors should issue a qualified opinion indicating that it is expressed except for the effects of the matter giving rise to the disagreement

3. An inherent uncertainty is an uncertainty whose resolution is dependent upon uncertain future events outside the control of the reporting entity's directors at the date the financial statements are approved.

    An inherent uncertainty is fundamental when the magnitude of its potential impact is so great that, without clear disclosure of the nature and implications of the uncertainty, the view given by the financial statements would be seriously misleading.

For example, where a large contract is up for renewal and the outcome is unknown at the date of approval of the financial statements, then it is an inherent uncertainty. If the outcome of the contract is vital to the continuing existence of the company then it would be fundamental. The auditor would then draw it to the attention of the readers of the financial statements in the audit report.

4. Four matters to consider prior to signing the audit report

- quality of audit work completed
- level of unadjusted differences
- results of file review and final analytical review of accounts
- results of completion of disclosure checklist
- have all outstanding items on the file been appropriately cleared
- appropriateness of opinion in relation to audit evidence obtained
- consistency and correctness of the wording of the report eg year end date correct, page number reference correct, correct reference to profit for year or loss for the year
- date of audit report
- letter of representation and the appropriateness of the representations received and signed by the directors approving the accounts
- quality and results of post balance sheet event work
- timing and coverage of post balance sheet event work to date of audit report

Task 3.1

Capital items included in repairs and maintenance – audit adjustment 1

Currently, fixed assets are understated by £/€28,441, being cost less depreciation charge. If the client does not agree to post this adjustment, it would not have any impact on the audit report since it is below materiality and computes as less than 5% of the loss for the year.

Incorrect depreciation charge – *audit adjustment 2*

Depreciation error of £/€11,132 is below materiality and would not have any impact on the audit report if not posted.

Motor vehicle recorded in the incorrect period – audit adjustment 3

This is simply a balance sheet reclass and since it is below materiality, non-posting should not have any effect on the audit report.

Insurance excess accrual – audit adjustment 4

Accruals are currently understated by £/€50k, however since this is below materiality and is less than 10% of the loss for the year, non-posting of this adjustment would not have any impact on the financial statements

Repairs and maintenance accrual – audit adjustment 5

This adjustment is not material and non-posting would not have any impact on the financial statements

Rebate accrual

The rebate accrual amounts to £/€150k which is above materiality. Presently, we do not have sufficient supporting documentation to form an opinion on this balance. As noted in the completion memo, we will be requesting further information and consider sending out confirmations to suppliers. Should we not get the appropriate back-up for this figure, we may have to consider a qualified opinion on the basis of limitation of scope.

Bad debt provision – audit adjustment 6

Currently trade debtors are overstated by £/€307,386. This error is very material. If the directors do not agree to post this journal, this would result in qualifying our audit report with an adverse opinion, due to the size of the adjustment.

Adjustments 1 to 5 individually do not have any impact on the audit report, if they are not posted both individually and in aggregate since the profit and loss impact in aggregate is immaterial at €6k. however, taking into account adjustment 6, an adverse opinion would be inserted in the audit